Cannabis for Greater Sexual Satisfaction

Discover Fun And Effective Ways To Spice up The Bedroom With Cannabis.

As cannabis is becoming more mainstream, research is confirming the impacts cannabis has on your libido. Cannabis, nature's aphrodisiac helps many overcome sexual shame and sexual difficulties. Resulting in better sex and orgasms.

In this revolutionary Itty Bitty Book, Carli Jo takes you down the path of possibilities by guiding you on how to pair cannabis and sex to create a happy, healthy sex life.

Introduce and play with these 15 ideas within your relationship to promote passion and erotic fun!

For example:

- Explore which form of cannabis is best for you.
- Create ritual for optimal pleasure.
- Learn your Core Erotic Blueprint™ type for greater sexual satisfaction.

Pick up a copy of this powerful book today and experience the joy that come when you invest in creating a loving, passion-filled sex life.

Your Amazing Itty Bitty® Guide to Cannabis and Sex

15 chapters on how to increase sexual satisfaction with cannabis

Carli Jo

Published by Itty Bitty® Publishing
A subsidiary of S & P Productions, Inc.

Copyright © 2020 Carli Jo

All rights reserved. No part of this book may be reproduced or transmitted in any form or by any means, electronic or mechanical, including photocopying, recording or by any information storage and retrieval system, without written permission of the publisher, except for inclusion of brief quotations in a review.

Printed in the United States of America

Itty Bitty Publishing
311 Main Street, Suite D
El Segundo, CA 90245
(310) 640-8885

ISBN: 978-1-950326-35-8

To my mother, who didn't disown me for writing this book. Thank you for always supporting me.

Stop by our Itty Bitty® website Directory to find interesting information about cannabis and sex.

www.IttyBittyPublishing.com

Or visit Carli Jo at:

Carlijo.com

Table of Contents

Introduction
- Step 1. Cannabis, A Sexual Tool
- Step 2. Cannabis To Increase Sexual Desire
- Step 3. Cannabis To Increase Sexual Health
- Step 4. Cannabis For Your Erotic Blueprint™
- Step 5. Cannabis And Sex
- Step 6. Cannabis And Self Pleasuring
- Step 7. Choosing Your Cannabis
- Step 8. Preparing Your Cannabis
- Step 9. Sacred Sexual Space
- Step 10. Cannabis Consumption Ritual
- Step 11. Pleasure Ritual #1
- Step 12. Pleasure Ritual #2
- Step 13. Pleasure Ritual #3
- Step 14. Elevated Orgasms
- Step 15. Sexy Cannabis Journal

Introduction

Welcome to your guide to all things sex and cannabis! The goal of this book is give you a basic understanding of how to use cannabis to enhance your sexual pleasure. As well as normalize the use of cannabis to increase sexual satisfaction.

I'm sure you've heard the hype on cannabis being an ally for having better sex. In this book you will discover how to choose, prepare and consume your cannabis. In addition you'll learn three practices to begin your journey today!

Each and every one of you has a unique pathway to pleasure and turn on. For some, cannabis is part of that path to greater arousal and better sex.

Tune in and get turned on!

Chapter 1
Cannabis, A Sexual Tool

Think of cannabis as another tool in your sexual toolbox, available to offer guidance and support on your path of sexual discovery.

1. Imagine that you have a sexy toolbox next to your bed and in that toolbox are items like your lubricant, dildo, vibrator, blindfold and furry handcuffs. Place cannabis in that sexy toolbox, viewing it as another tool for increasing sexual pleasure.
2. This helps remove the shame and guilt of "needing" cannabis to feel sexually turned on.
3. Instead right here right now make a commitment to accepting cannabis as a tool for showing you what is possible.
4. Any and all discoveries of tools for greater pleasure are worthy of celebration!

Using cannabis in an intentional way for increasing sexual desire.

Before you can start using cannabis to enhance your sex life, you must first understand that cannabis is:

- natural.
- an herb, not a weed.
- medicinal, not a drug.
- a gateway to healing not to drugs.

Cannabis has medicinal and spiritual benefits that can aid in elevating your mind, body and mood. Cannabis:

- allows blood flow to the frontal lobe, which helps you open up your creative center.
- allows blood to flow to your sexual organs and genitals, increasing arousal.
- increases spiritual growth and enlightenment.
- allows for deeper presence.

Chapter 2
Cannabis To Increase Sexual Desire

Cannabis can be a wonderful ally for improving your sex life. When used responsibly and intentionally it can help increase sexual desire by elevating your mood.

1. The most common issues that keep you out of your sexuality are caused by stress, anxiety, or depression. These issues can lead to "performance anxiety," emotional distance, and low libido.
2. Cannabis can help you overcome these issues because of its powerful effects on both your body and your mind.
3. Cannabis can increase sensitivity and awareness to pleasure, creating peace in your body and by lowering inhibitions.
4. Cannabis can reduce over active thinking in your frontal lobe, allowing you to be more in your body and less in your head.
5. Cannabis is nature's aphrodisiac.

Tips for Conscious Consumption

Set the intention for cannabis to increase sexual desire then allow the plant medicine to flow throughout your body.

- Cannabis affects everyone differently.
- Not every experience will be the same.
- Try being patient with yourself and your sexuality.
- Give your body permission to experience what is needed.

Sexual pleasure can come in many different forms. It can be:

- Erotic
- Sexual
- Playful
- Lustful
- Meditative
- Restorative
- Relaxing
- Sexy

Chapter 3
Cannabis To Increase Sexual Health

Sexual health is just as important as physical health and mental health but isn't viewed as important in western culture. When you take time out of your week to focus on your sex life, you increase your sexual vibrancy and health.

Benefits of making your sexual health a priority:

1. The more you have sex the more you want sex, improving your libido.
2. Sex increases vitality, keeping you feeling and looking younger.
3. More sex can equal longer lasting and more intense orgasms.
4. Sex lowers blood pressure.
5. Greater intimacy and lower divorce rate.
6. Sex improves sleep.
7. Sex gives you a deeper connection to yourself as well as to your partner.
8. Sex strengths pelvic floor muscles.

Cannabis for sexual health

Cannabis has been known to decrease, heal and eliminate the following issues/symptoms:

- Endometriosis
- Erectile Dysfunction
- Vulvadenia (pain during sex)
- Dryness
- Pelvic pain
- Irregular periods
- Menstrual cramps
- Menopause

Cannabis infused suppositories are designed to be inserted vaginally or anally to deliver a dose of THC/CBD which can help:

- Lower PMS symptoms
- Heal endometriosis
- Decrease inflammation and pain
- Increase wetness
- Increase relaxation
- Elevate mood

Chapter 4
Cannabis For Your Erotic Blueprint™

The Erotic Blueprints are a framework for better understanding how your desire and arousal works. Therefore giving you the language to talk about your sexuality with greater ease and acceptance.

Miss Jaiya, the creator the Erotic Blueprints discovered five sexual archetypes to help you better understand and accept your individual path to pleasure.

The 5 Erotic Blueprint types are:

1. Energetic: Turned on by anticipation, tease and yearning.
2. Sensual: Turned on by all five senses activated.
3. Sexual: Turned on by penetration, nudity and orgasms.
4. Kinky: Turned on by anything considered "taboo."
5. Shapeshifter: Turned on by it all and wants it all.

Cannabis for your Erotic Blueprint

Understanding your Erotic Blueprint helps you best pair cannabis for your unique sexual wiring.

Some examples of pairings are:

Energetic
- Low dose edibles, 2-5 mg.
- Balanced strains with lower amounts of THC.

Sensual
- THC/CBD infused bath.
- Relaxing strains with intoxicating flavors/smells.

Sexual
- THC/CBD infused personal lubricants.
- Mood boosting strains high in THC.

Kinky
- THC/CBD infused massage lotions.
- CBD dominant strains that boost creativity.

Shapeshifter
- Variety is key.
- Consider a combo of the above mentioned.

Visit Carlijo.com/quiz to discover your Cannabis For Greater Sexual Satisfaction.

Chapter 5
Cannabis And Sex

Inviting cannabis into your sex life with a partner can be a fun and helpful way to elevate your experience.

1. Cannabis can increase your sexual desires by increasing sensitivity to pleasure by lowering sexual challenges.
2. Cannabis can induce creativity allowing sex and pleasure to be more wild, fun, erotic and/or playful.
3. Creating a cannabis ritual can bring the excitement back into sex.
4. Cannabis can increase your ability to have longer lasting and more enjoyable orgasms.
5. Cannabis can increase the longevity of sexual experiences.
6. Cannabis induces the impairment of short-term memory, which is helpful for keeping the focus on sex.
(thegrowthop.com)

Just you, cannabis and me

The days of consuming before sex are over. Try bringing cannabis into the bedroom for a fun and intimate date night.

- Dosage is crucial for pairing cannabis and sex, especially since large doses affect performance.
- Try consuming low amounts of THC or micro dosing which is when you start off with one hit or one bite, see how you feel then add more when desired.

If you desire the medicinal effects of cannabis without the high:

- There are a lot of potential sexual benefits to using CBD, but one of the most notable is the cannabinoid's potential to help with erectile dysfunction. This is largely due to its ability to repair tissue damage and improve blood flow to the genitals. CBD is also known for its ability to naturally boost one's energy and being a stress reliever.

Cannabis infused lubricant

- Is a great choice for receiving the benefits of cannabis without the euphoric head high commonly associated with consuming THC.

Chapter 6
Cannabis And Self-Pleasuring

Sexual enjoyment has a variety of factors that depend on the individual and even the day. Inviting cannabis into your personal exploration can be helpful way to better understand your pleasure. Self-pleasure is:

1. Anything that gives you pleasure.
2. Touch of skin, brushing of hair, a bubble bath.
3. Genital stimulation.
4. Breast/chest massage/touching.

Having a regular self-pleasuring practice can:

1. Increase confidence, self-awareness and self-empathy.
2. Release dopamine and oxytocin.
3. Increase your self-love and sense of well-being.
4. Help you better understand your body and desires.
5. Support inner balance.
6. Orgasms can reduce stress levels, aging, anxiety and depression.

Self-pleasuring for spiritual connection:

- Turn self-pleasure into a time of deep connection and intimacy with yourself.
- Helps develop a greater connection to self-love & self-acceptance.
- Creates relaxation and a surrendered state of openness and free-flow of energy through the body.
- Is like eating healthy, organic food for your brain.
- Expand into new areas of pleasure.

Pleasure Meditation:

- Play with cannabis in self-pleasure so you can learn how it affects your level of arousal.
- Try focusing on your breath, deep inhales and relaxed exhales.
- When relaxed, slowly begin to incorporate touch.
- Breathe into the skin on skin contact.
- Breathe into the sensations and pleasure.

Chapter 7
Choosing Your Cannabis

Cannabis comes in many varieties. Ideally you want to experiment with what works for you and what doesn't. The only way to know is try!

- Edibles (gummies, brownie, mints…) work by metabolizing through the liver, which is why the effects are unpredictable.
- Tinctures are the oral administration of liquid cannabis extract. Tinctures can take up to 30 minutes to two hours to take effect.
- Vaporizer pens heat the herb to a temperature that is high enough to extract THC. Great option for those wanting to be discreet or want to minimize the odor.
- Flower can be smoked in paper, pipes or vaporizers.

Best strains for sex

There are a wide variety of cannabis strains that offer a spectrum of medicinal benefits. Which means choosing the best strain of cannabis for sex is just as individual as the plant itself.

Indica, Sativa and CBD

According to mainstream cannabis culture, there are two distinct groups: Indica and Sativa. However, recent research shows that there's little to no evidence that all indicas and all sativas have a common effect.

Try experimenting with this guideline:

- THC-dominant strains have higher euphoric qualities, which cause the "high" feeling. Great for lowering anxiety and depression.
- CBD-dominant strains contain less amounts of THC and more CBD. CBD is non psychoactive. CBD is great for lowering or eliminating stress, which is a major cause of reduced sexual desire.
- Balanced THC/CBD strains offer a balanced dose. Great for beginners or those seeking a light "high."

Chapter 8
Preparing Your Cannabis

No matter if you're alone or with a partner, proper planning prevents poor partying. In this case the party is your body and sexuality!

1. Choose your method of consumption.
2. Gather any devices needed such as your pipe, rolling papers and/or lighter.
3. Understand, read and learn about the cannabis you choose. Such as it's strain, potency and time delay of affects.
4. Choose your desired dosing.
5. Have a glass of water on hand.

Cannabis Ritual

For setting up a mindful cannabis ritual to enhance your sexuality - roll yourself a senusal joint.

- Note that this ritual can be done with any cannabis modality (edible, tincture, sublingual) but is described with flower.
- There is something very grounding about the act of grinding your flower & rolling your joint. It really connects you to the plant.
- Intentionality is key.
- Really being present to the process of preparing for your ritual adds a mindful awareness.
- Set an intention for your practice then place that energy into your flower as you prepare it.

Chapter 9
Setting Up Your Sacred Sensual Space

To invite the utmost intimacy and relaxation, the first step in your ritual should be to create a sacred sensual space. This is essential to the development of your sexuality and self-expression. It should invite exploration and ignite pleasure.

1. Choose a space that is quiet with little to no distractions or interruptions.
2. Intentionally create a soothing, sexy environment that satisfies all five of your senses.
3. Candles or aromatic oils
4. Pillows & blankets
5. Soft music
6. Crystal or sacred objects
7. Plant medicine (tea, cannabis, cacao, etc.)
8. Skin friendly oils for lubricants
9. Water

Sanctify your sacred sensual experience by:

- Step into your sacred space for a minimum of 10 minutes.
- Place one hand on your heart and one hand on your belly to help align your body and mind as you ground yourself into your new space.
- Say or visualize your intention, "I am now in my sacred sexual space."
- This is your time for you.

Once you're all set up and this make take some time; stay curious and change your set up whenever it feels right.

Chapter 10
Cannabis Consumption Ritual

Connecting to the plant medicine is very grounding and when done intentionally can be used as a spiritual guide. You'll want to begin by setting an intention for your session. Have a clear and intentional reason for bringing cannabis into your practice. Some examples are:

1. My intention is to be present.
2. My intention is to experience the greatest pleasure possible.
3. My intention is to heal.
4. My intention is to allow cannabis to show me what is possible in my sexuality.

Pairing intimacy and cannabis

When it comes to pairing sexual intimacy and cannabis, you don't want to over do it by getting too high, paranoid or passing out. Consider these effective ways to ensure a positive experience:

- Starting with CBD. CBD has many of the same benefits of THC but without the high.
- Try strains high in CBD and low in THC.
- Practice micro dosing. Micro dosing is taking small doses; waiting 20-30 minutes then see how you feel before consuming more.
- Avoid mixing cannabis and alcohol.
- When consuming with edibles take into consideration that it takes time to get high and then getting over being high.
- Be patient. Finding the right dose can take time.

How to smoke cannabis

- Inhale slowly for a count of 1, 2, 3
- Hold the breath in for 1, 2
- Exhale slowly for 3, 2, 1

Sit and see how you feel. Remember that you can always have more but you can't take it away. Timing will depend on method of consumption. Edibles for example can take 30-60 minutes before effects kick in. Repeat as desired.

Chapter 11
Pleasure Ritual #1: Body Meditation

This body mediation is designed to help you tune in and connect with your body, sensations, and emotions. Noticing the arising sensations is key to understanding how cannabis affects your body.

A few keys points:

1. There's no wrong way to do this as long as you're doing it!
2. Use the power of your breath to turn your focus inward.
3. If your mind starts to wander, bring the focus back to your body using your breath.
4. Try repeating, "I am present" out loud.
5. Practice body meditations as often as possible.

Relax, Relax, Relax!

Once you've chosen & prepped your cannabis and set up your sacred sensual space you are ready to explore.

- Step in your sacred sensual space.
- Set an intention for this practice.
- Connect to your cannabis using the Consumption Ritual from chapter 10.
- Lie down, get comfortable and begin to focus on your breathing.
- Inhaling deeply through the nose, relaxed exhales out through the mouth.
- Repeat as necessary until you're feeling in your body.

When ready:
- Scan your body from the tips of your toes to the crown of your head, noticing any arising sensations, moment-to-moment.
- Say out loud what you're noticing and where you're experiencing it. Examples: itch in my nose, tingle in my elbow, and warmth in my heart.
- Keep going until you feel complete.

Chapter 12
Pleasure Ritual #2: Pleasure Circuit

This Pleasure Ritual is designed to identify and expand sexual pleasure throughout your body.

1. Start by lying down or sitting with your spine straight.
2. Inhaling deeply through the nose, relaxed exhales out of the mouth.
3. Repeat as necessary until you feel relaxed and in your body.
4. Scan your body, noticing where you feel good, where you feel pleasure.
5. Once located, focus your awareness into this space, breathing in and out.
6. Notice if there is a color, shape or sensation in this space.
7. With your breath and awareness, see if you can expand this pleasure, making it bigger and/or brighter.

Pleasure, Pleasure, Pleasure!

As you feel the pleasure expand in your body consider the following to increase the experience:

- Set an intention for this practice.
- Connect to your cannabis using the Consumption Ritual from chapter 10.
- Consider adding pleasure by touching, stroking or massaging your body/genitals.
- Repeat as often as possible for greater awareness of pleasure!

Complete this practice by lying in stillness. Bring one hand to your heart and place one hand on your genitals. Thank your body for the pleasure experienced.

Chapter 13
Pleasure Ritual #3: Presence For Increased Pleasure (partnered exercise)

One of the biggest challenges you face during sex is the inability to get out of your head. Cannabis, paired with presence practices, can induce the impairment of short-term memory, which is suitable for staying present during sex.

1. Begin this practice seated at the edge of the bed with your partner, facing one another.
2. Follow steps for Cannabis Consumption Ritual from Chapter 10.
3. Set your intentions together or separately out loud to one another.
4. Once finished begin the grounding ritual for increased connection.

Grounding Ritual:

Great practice for couples to experience deeper presence.

- Gently close your eyes and drop into your own body.
- Inhale deeply through the nose and relaxed exhales out of the mouth.
- Repeat as necessary until you're feeling in your body.

Yes, Yes, Yes!

When feeling relaxed and centered, open your eyes and gaze into one another's left eye. Set a timer for two minutes.

Left eye gazing comes from the Tantric tradition and its benefits include:

- An opportunity to become present and experience the true essence of another.
- When it feels confrontational, eye gazing helps boost our confidence, improves self-esteem and develops self-awareness.
- It can deepen intimacy. Helping partners feel more connected.

Once a deeper sense of relaxation and connection is felt, flow into intimacy.

Chapter 14
Elevated Orgasms

Cannabis has been known to allow direct concentration and focus to a specific task. In this process allow that task to be an Elevated Orgasm.

1. When cannabis is paired with meditation, intention and focus, the ability to be present can increase.
2. Being present and feeling grounded with a relaxed and openhearted presence allows heightened states of awareness for greater pleasure.
3. Shutting off the chatter of the monkey mind while focusing on the arising sensations felt in your body can assist in increasing your experience.
4. When fueled by love and compassion, orgasmic energy can be felt throughout the entire body.
5. Orgasms have multiple potential health benefits due to the hormones and chemicals released by the body during an orgasm.

Oh my!

Some effects cannabis can have on the body.

- Tingling
- Warmth
- Excitement
- Euphoria
- Mood enhancement
- Increased arousal

There is very little research on cannabis enhancing orgasm, however, it's coming! If you're turned on by facts then this section is for you!

Fact #1: Cannabis is a vasodilator, meaning it opens blood vessels and increases blood flow to your genitals.

Fact #2: The psychoactive effect of THC happens when dopamine floods the brain increasing the feeling of pleasure and joy.

Fact #3: The more relaxed you are the higher the awareness on things feeling better. Better chances of an orgasm!

Chapter 15
Sexy Cannabis Journal

Keeping a journal of your experiences with cannabis and sex is a great way to track your likes and dislikes. Use a blank page journal or a notebook of any kind.

1. Recording your cannabis consumption is a great way to help you maximize the effects of pairing cannabis and sex. Different strains impact everyone differently as well as usage-to-usage.
2. Before you begin, I suggest journaling about your day, current mood and anything that might hinder your experience.
3. This journal will come in very handy the next time you have to choose your cannabis!

Information and how to organize it:

- Date
- Form (vape, edibles, flower etc.)
- Strain Name: (Granddaddy Purple, Sour Diesel, Lemon Kush etc.)
- Current mood
- Intention for consuming
- Effects: How did it make you feel?
    - Aroused
    - Paranoid
    - Hungry
    - Relaxed

- Recap: Jot down any notes that you have and want to remember from this experience.

Visit Carlijo.com/journal to download Carli Jo's Sexy Cannabis Journal.

You've finished. Before you go…

Tweet/share that you finished this book.

Please star rate this book.

Reviews are solid gold to writers. Please take a few minutes to give us some itty bitty feedback.

ABOUT THE AUTHOR

Carli Jo is a Cannabis Sensuality Coach specializing in helping individuals learn their Erotic Blueprint™ Type for a deeper understanding of their unique sexual wiring and pathway to pleasure.

Carli Jo's cutting edge work has been featured in The New Yorks Times, Merry Jane Media and High Times Magazine.

When Carli Jo is not working on her Sex and Cannabis business she enjoys spending time with her dog Chester and husband Jose who lets him be her guinea pig.

If you enjoyed this Itty Bitty® book you might also like…

- **Your Amazing Itty Bitty® Marijuana Manual** – Kat Bohnsack

- **Your Amazing Itty Bitty® Guide to Cannabis** – Hyla Cass, MD and Mikaila Kemp

- **Your Amazing Itty Bitty® Have More Sex Book** – Jan Robinson

Or any of the other Itty Bitty® books available on line.

www.ingramcontent.com/pod-product-compliance
Lightning Source LLC
Chambersburg PA
CBHW061305040426
42444CB00010B/2529